Rhyme
& Reason

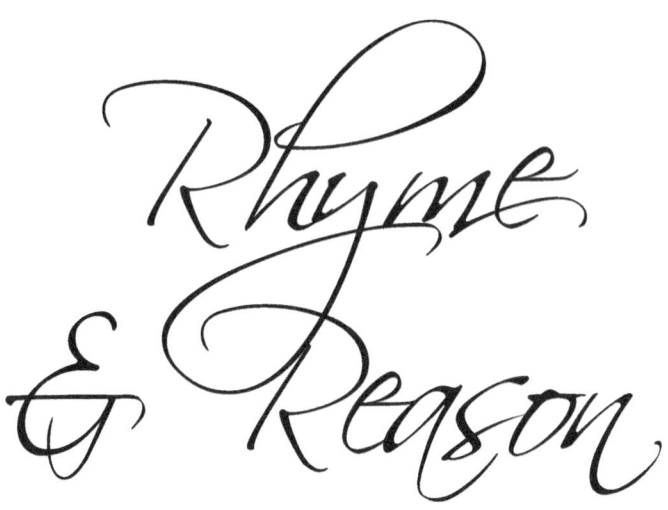

April A. VanApeldorn

Library of Congress Control Number: 2021923381
ISBN: Hardcover   978-1-6641-9796-1
               Softcover   978-1-6641-9795-4
               eBook   978-1-6641-9794-7

Print information available on the last page.

Rev. date: 11/18/2021

To order additional copies of this book, contact:
Xlibris
844-714-8691
www.Xlibris.com
Orders@Xlibris.com
836149

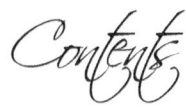

Contents

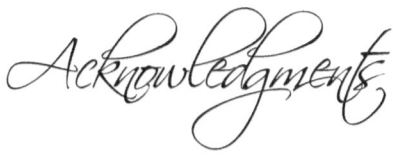

Acknowledgments

I would like give a special thank you to my mother, April Bruni Sr., for her continuous support, love, strength and for her amazing artwork collaboration on this book.

A big thank you to my best friend, James Spooner, for his never-ending motivation, honesty, and for always being my cheerleader.

Last but not least, a humble thank you to Taleah & Ryan Valles-Peters, Patience Taka, and Beau Sherman for your help with bringing this to life.

To my youth, my life experiences, dear friends, those lost but not forgotten and the vast world around me, thank you. Thank you for the journey full of memories, laughter, pain and lessons learned that help create the words within this book as well as the woman I am today.

Mr. Wrong

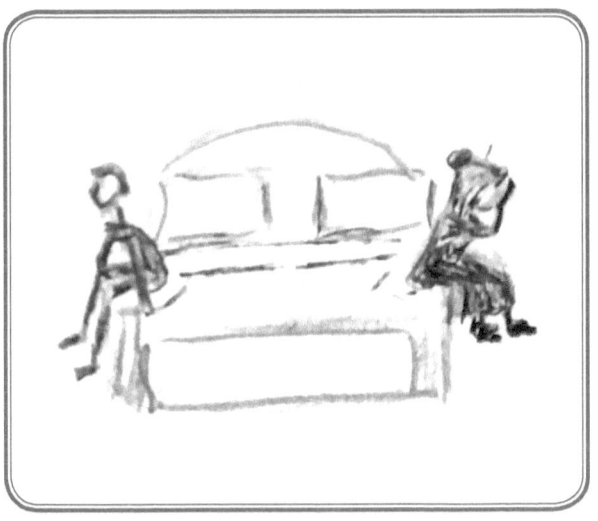

You say you want a love so true
You just want Mr. Right
But all you do is just argue
The two of you just love to fight
He cheats and lies
She gets mad and cries
But never does it get better
He'll do it again with a smile this time
She'll cuss and throw a fit
Yet they get back together like a baby to a tit
The cycle continues till hate fills their heart
There will be no till death do us part
End this chapter … why stay?
Mr. Right can't find you until you walk away

Mirage

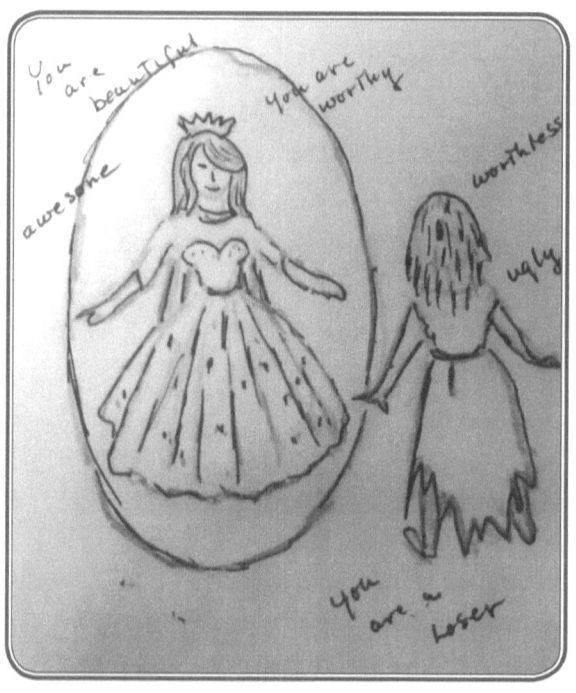

Living inside a mirage
Actions speak words so loud
Motions are screams in a crowd
It's an emotional sabotage
Walk through the portal to the other side
Speak words not filled with pride
Open your heart, open it now
Trust yourself, I know you know how

Get It Done

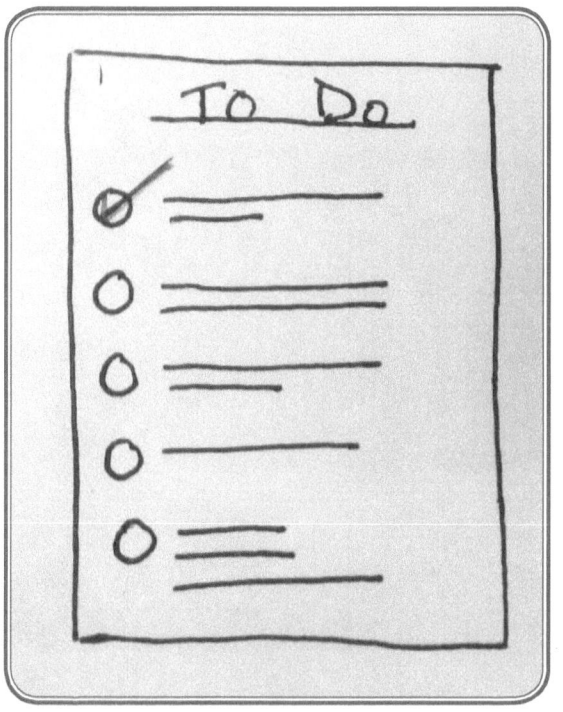

Back into the daily grind
So much to do, so little time
Everything rushing through my mind
Completion has been set in stone
Cannot accomplish this alone
Grab my troops and hit the ground
To the finish we are bound
Battle of the clock has begun
Together we will get it done.

Forever Pain

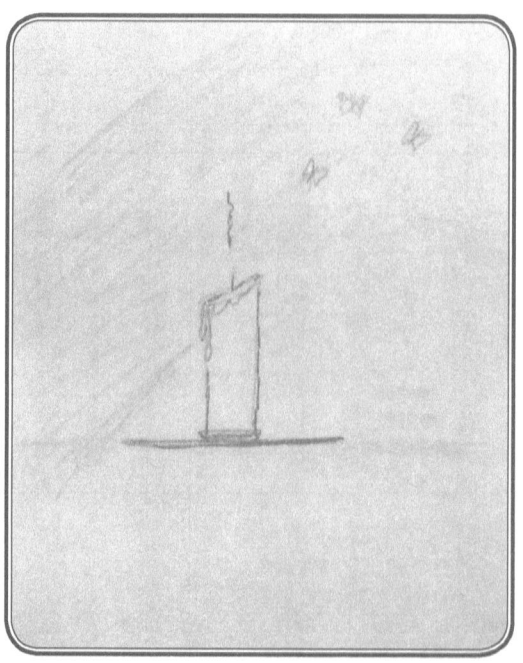

Perched surrounded by a thousand thread counts
Lying in her resting place
The sky has blackened by the night
Her beatbox swirls within her stomach like the churning of the sea
Anxious nerves dance through her veins to the drums of her pounding head
Moths flutter around her soul searching for the light
The light that is no more
Blown out by life's unexpected wind
Replaced by an open sore
A sore that in time will no longer show
But the pain it has caused she will forever know

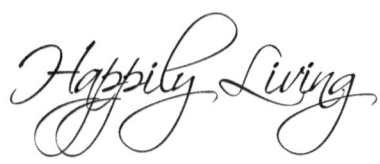

Happily Living

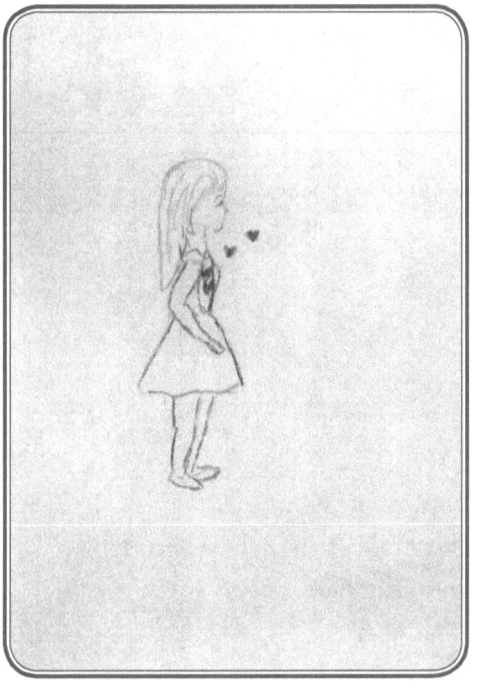

The empty hole deep inside
The peg that fits is not pride
Packing it full of material things
Burying it with meaningless flings
A temporary fix is all that brings
Surround the heart with those you love
Spend some time with the one above
Though this may sound very sappy
It's in those moments you'll be truly happy

Decision Made

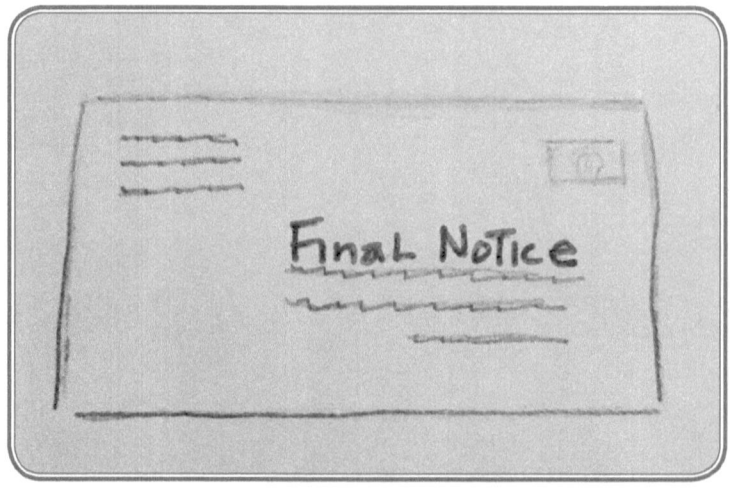

Decision made, I thought it through
It was a tough one
Not looking good for you
It is set and now it's done
A new journey has begun
You may not get it, but have no fear
I made the decision; my mind is clear

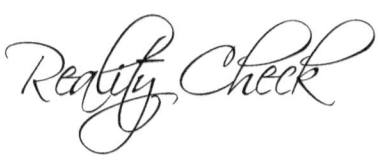

Reality Check

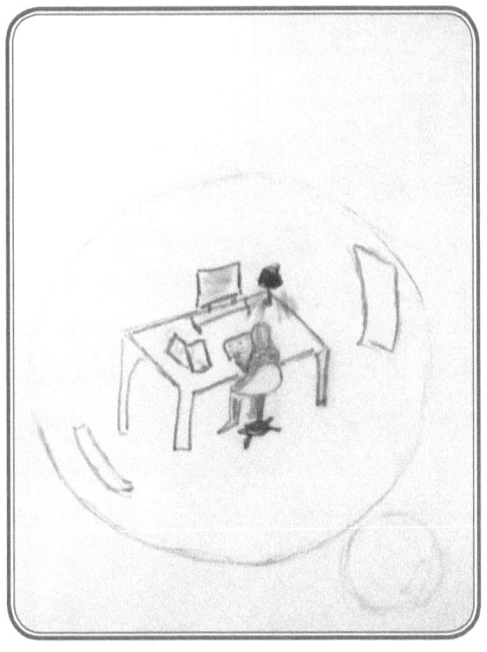

Your world is virtual
There is no reality
Living via the internet
Hiding behind a screen for a safety net
Alone and sad but not sure why
As you're letting the world pass you by
But you go ahead, stay inside your bubble
It won't be there when there are signs of trouble
But if you'd only look up from the keyboard
You would see you are loved and so adored

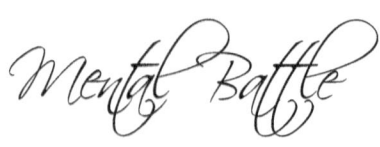

Mental Battle

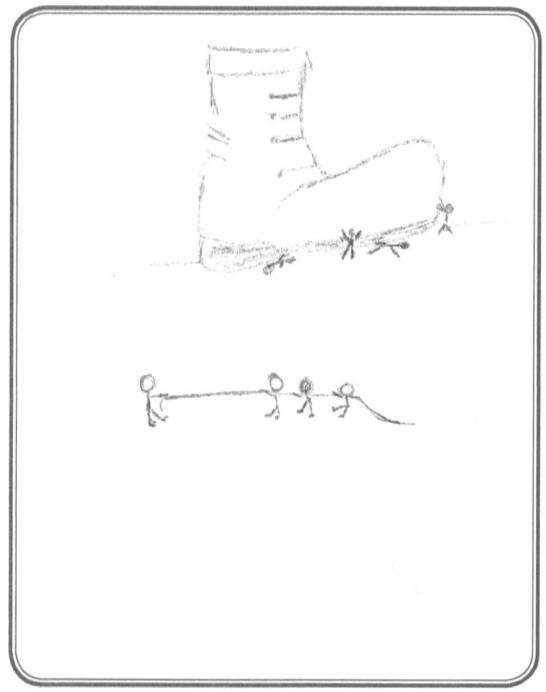

A self-inflicted mental bruise
Battle within the mind
Is this all just a ruse?
Beware of what you'll find
Visions causing brain destruction
Striving for mind reconstruction
Peace has become a rarity
But all I need is some simple clarity.

Darker Side

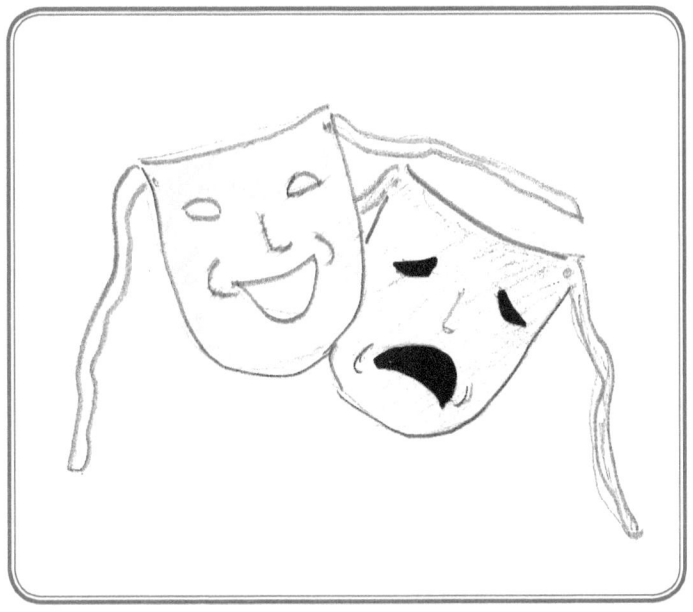

Dear darker side of me
you need to lighten up
though life may be up and down
it doesn't mean that I will drown
pain in my veins but a smile on my face
by inner determination, I complete the race
Dear darker side of me,
you will not take a toll
my life thrives through positivity
to which you have no role

Commissioned

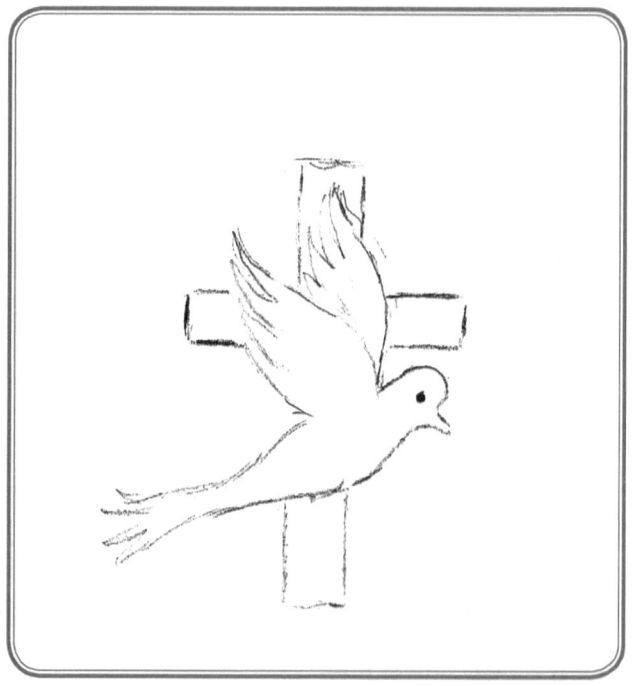

You heard clearly his voice
With no hesitation, made your choice
Though this is not your life's dream
You knew you belong on his team
You have made a difference, can't you see?
So many lives you've helped set free
And though from this path you wanted to stray
We are so glad you trusted to stay
You chose to follow and you listened
And now today, you are commissioned

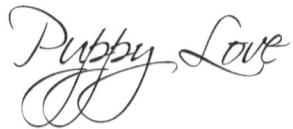

Puppy Love

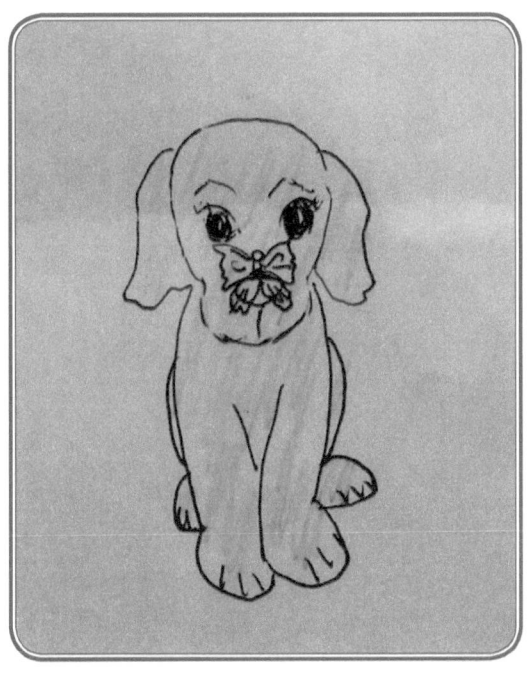

No matter if my day's insane
You always greet me just the same
Eyes so full of joy
A wagging tail says "Oh boy!"
Happy feet dancing all about
Your little bark gives a loving shout
With cuddles and wet kisses
Tells it's me that he misses
Oh how I can't get enough of
His never-changing puppy love

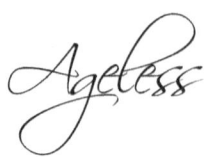

Ageless

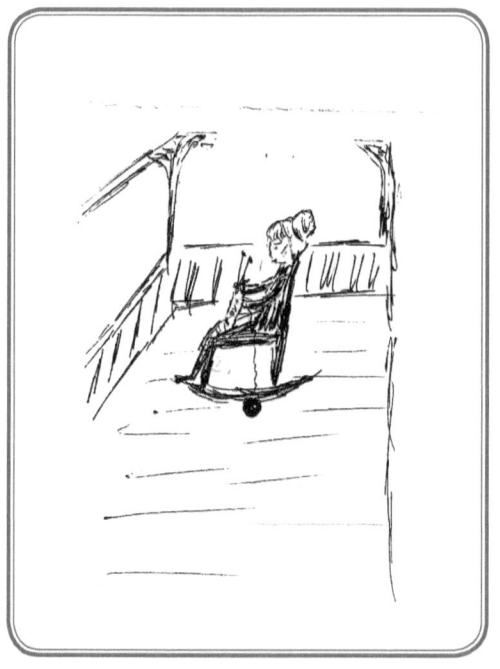

I watch you sway in your chair
Light glistening on your silver hair
Your skin bearing each life-earned scar
Your mind wanders somewhere afar
Oh the stories your eyes do tell
Of a life full of learning that all ends well
Finding your purpose, you lived cageless
So now, your words are forever ageless

Transparent Truth

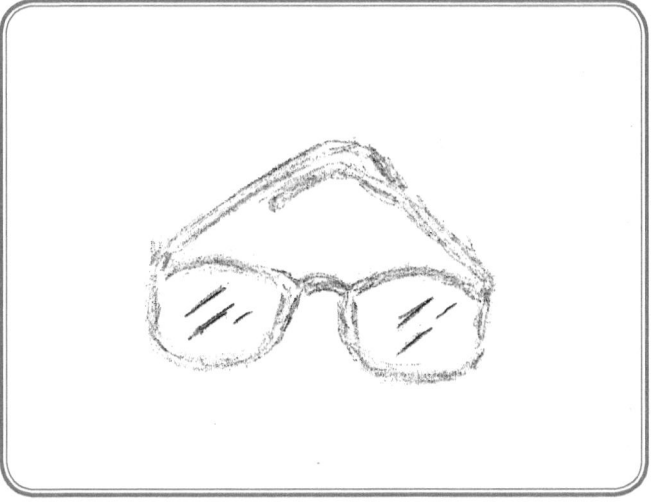

Waves over waves crash upon my eyes
a life filled with foolish lies
honesty, how hard it is to come
to show our soul to someone
our flaws make up our very being
but we tell a story to all who are seeing
it's OK to not be perfect
in a world so filled with every defect
be truthful about who you are
only you can set that bar

Self-Oppression

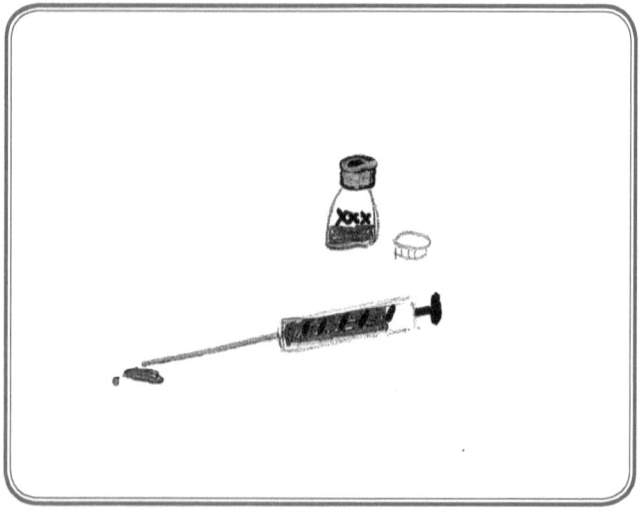

No energy inside
lost my youthful pride
all daily tasks, a chore
life in general, a bore
no motivation for it
no inner fire lit
unhappiness to the core
yet wanting something more
can't seem to shake the feeling
because nothing seems appealing
keeping asking myself why
while in silence I do lie

Determination

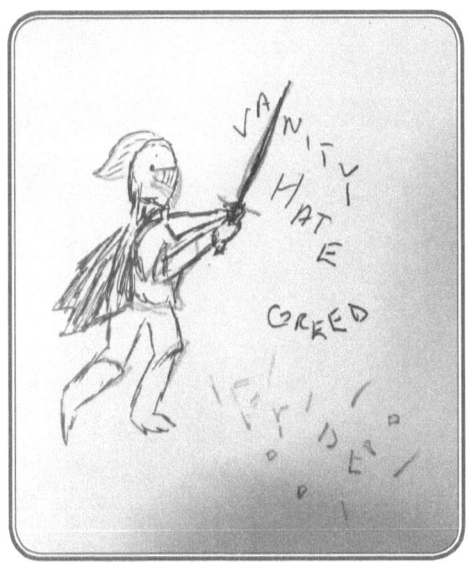

The hardest times can fall on my shoulders
Taking my breath away
Like a thousand pounds of boulders
Do I run, or do I stay?
The lines of worry dress my face
A heart beating at a jogger's pace
Stand up tall in the midst of gray
Dust off the demons seeking my mind like prey
Won't believe that I will fail
It's all in my mind, a self-made tale
This moment soon will disappear
The answer is so very clear
Determination is all I know
Step up and fight
Don't run … Don't go

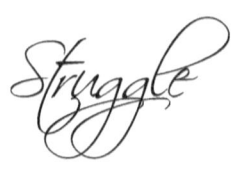

Struggle

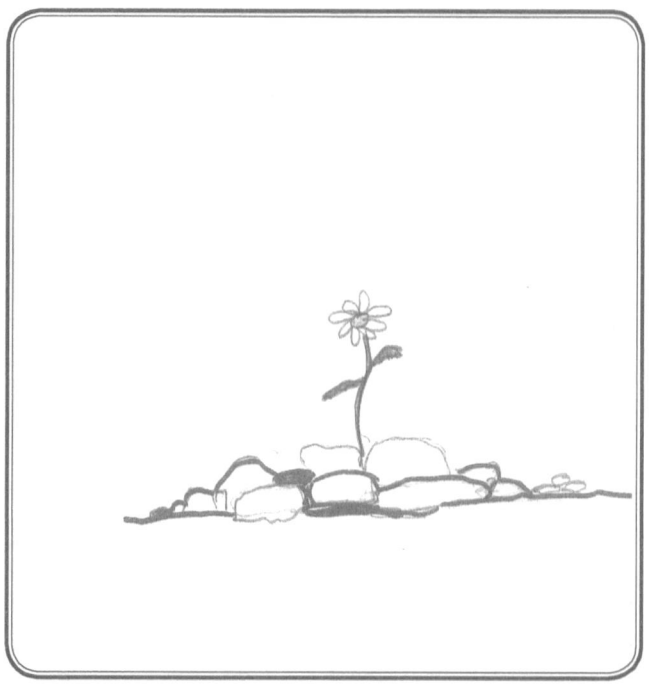

I don't know where to start
I know this hurts your heart
I say I want to follow you
But then I walk away
All signs that have come from you
Are begging me to stay
The desires of my flesh are weak
I struggle even as I speak
I cannot take a stand
Unless you take my hand
You promised you won't let me go
And I do have faith; this you already know

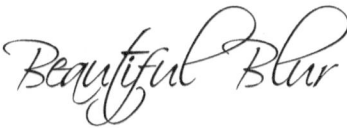

Beautiful Blur

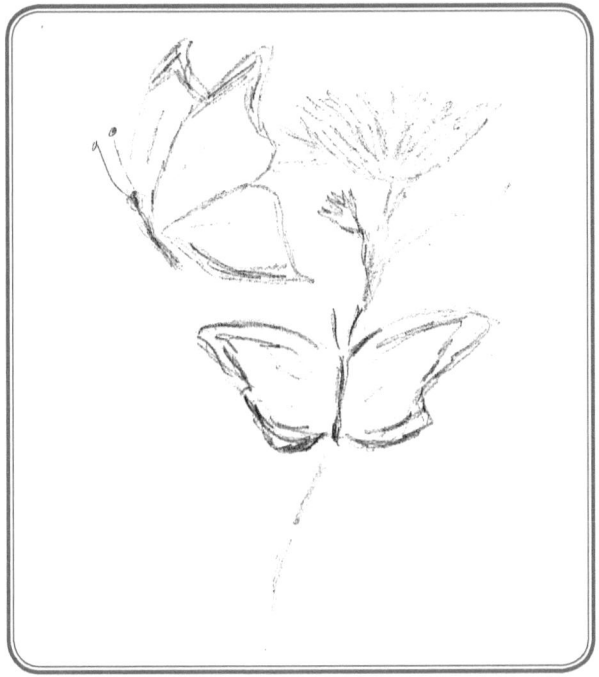

The horizon is a beautiful blur full of amazing possibilities. The mirror of memories shattered below your feet … no looking back. Lean into the wind … float upon the sea … open up your mind … only then will you be free.

The wings of life glide through each day of breath like butterflies grazing a garden.

Colors burst so glorious like precious moments of happiness. A smile or an embrace that consumes your every thought.

Eyes of the soul speak through the heart …

Be true … be you … that is where it starts.

Time's Up

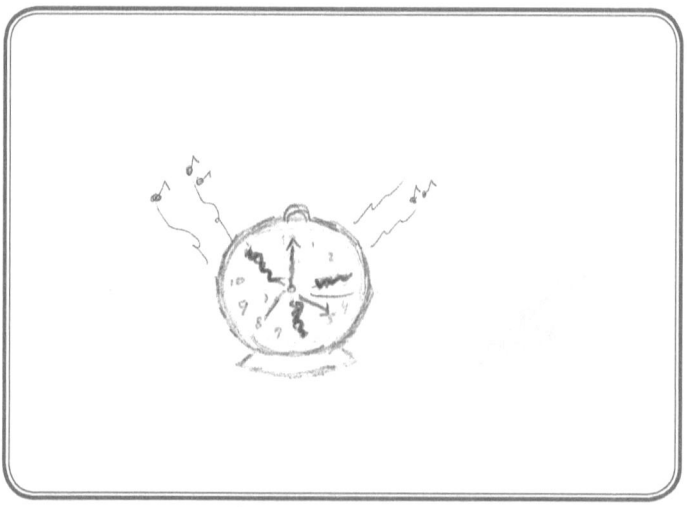

The clock has stopped ticking
That moment is the past
Time was of the essence
Yet it went by so fast
White flag has been thrown
Not much else to say
Not giving up, just moving on
Must go a different way

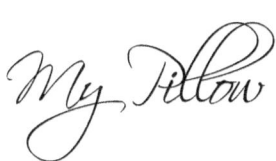

My Pillow

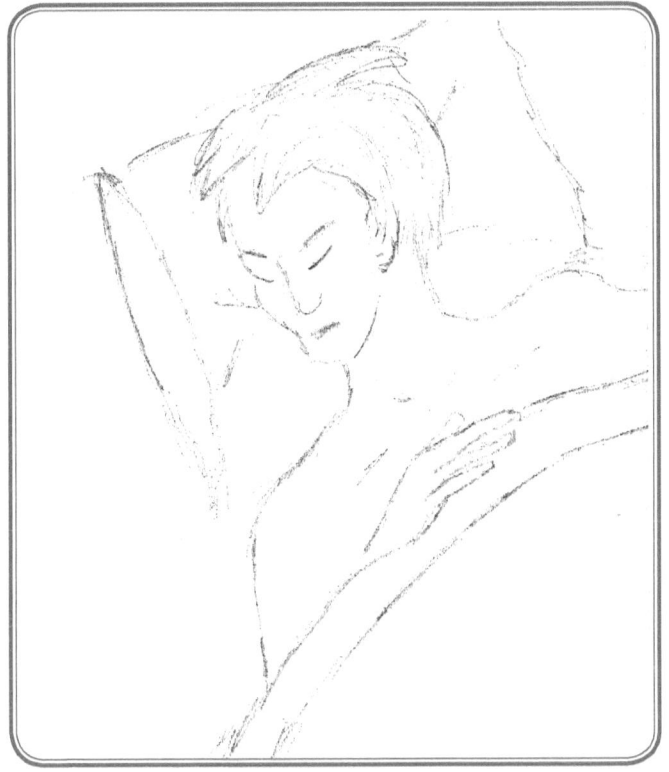

Soft, fluffy, puffy delight
Lift my dreams into flight
Cradle my thoughts in your nest
Protect my head as I rest
Hold me close as I reset my mind
Comfort me as my brain unwinds
Full of airy feathers, oh so light
My soft, fluffy, puffy delight

Dancing Waters

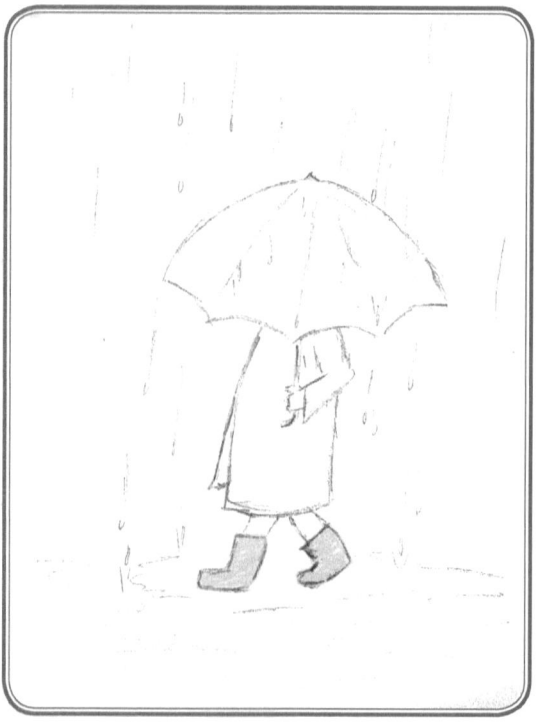

Water dances from the sky
Falling steadily from heaven's eye
Glistening happily all around
Shining on the darkened ground
Flowing waters full of grace
Dripping all over my face
Swirling down into the night
Sounds so peaceful, making everything right

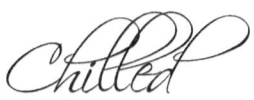

Chilled

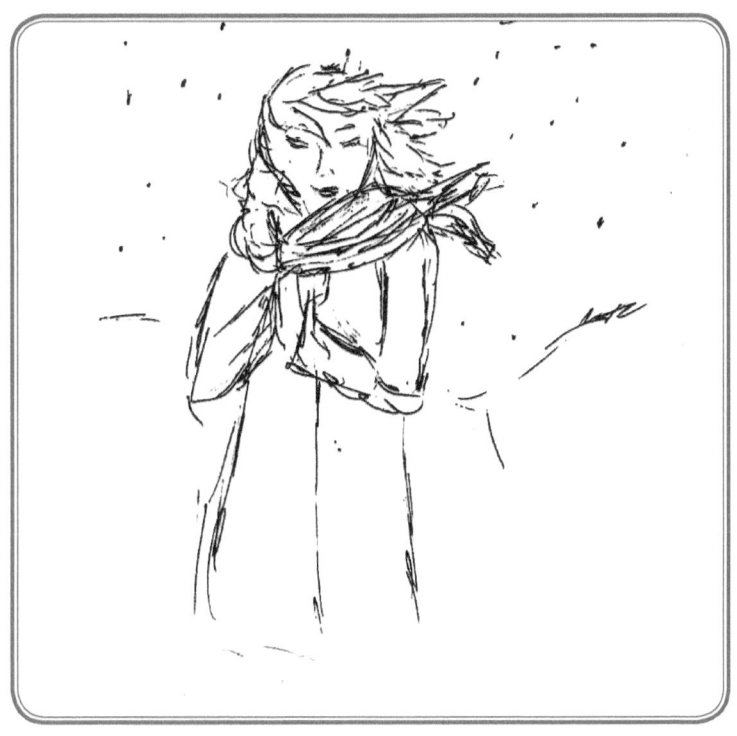

My body shivers
My lips quiver
As the cold air hits my skin
I grasp the warmth that is within
The breeze blows through my hair
A crisp chill in the air
Mother Nature shuns the sun
For winter has begun

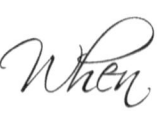

When

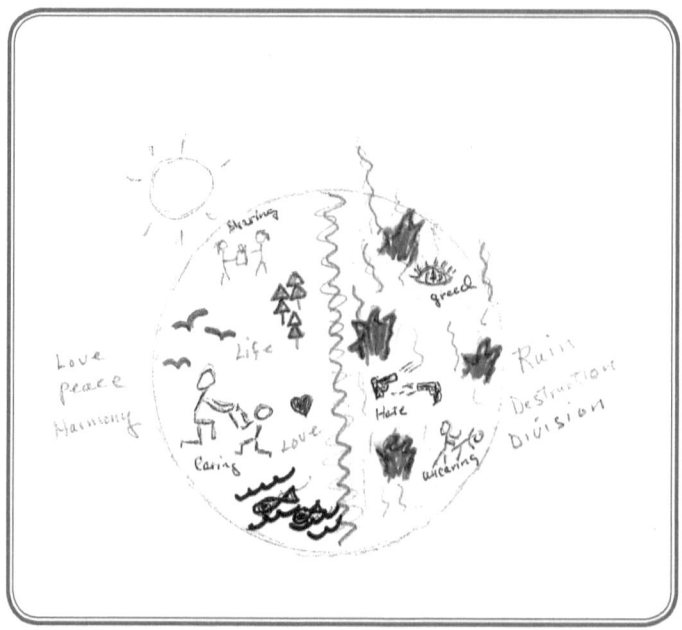

When did we stop loving each other?
When did we start causing pain?
When did we become so selfish?
When did we become so vain?
When did we stop caring for others?
When did it become about self-gain?
When did we stop going the extra mile?
When did we start wanting a virtual smile?
Why did we give Satan the wheel
When he only came to destroy, lie, and steal?
For God so loved the world ...
When will we?

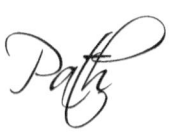

Path

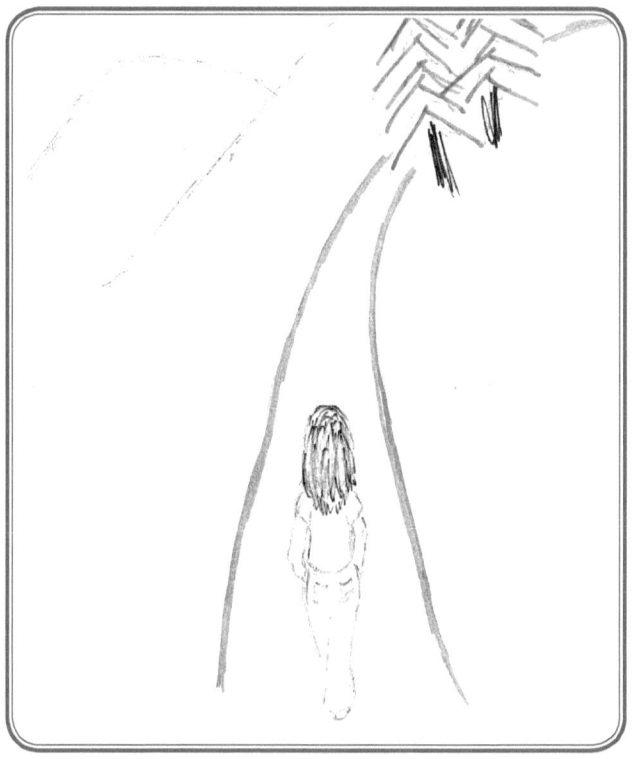

The road I'm on I walk alone
I pave it as I go
Though I stop along my way
On this road I will stay
Its destination is untold
No one follows on my path
For my journey can't re-unfold

Love So Soft

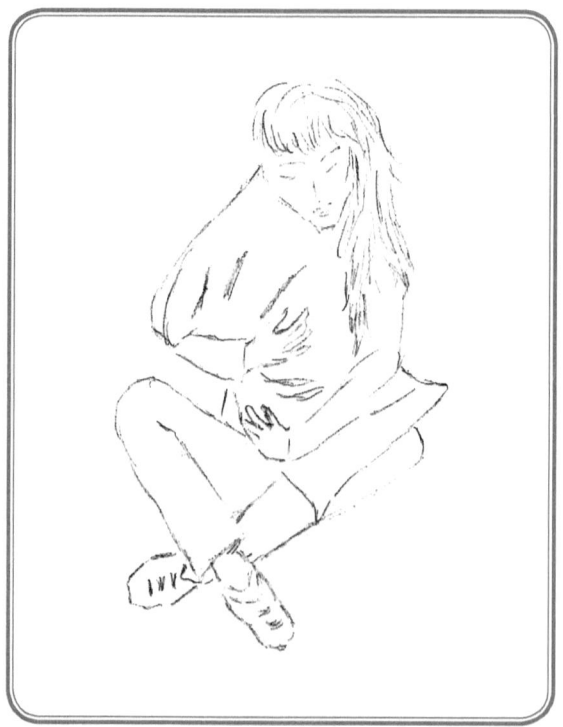

True love is like a pillow.
You can hug it when you're in trouble.
You can cry on it when you're in pain.
You can embrace it when you're happy.
So when you need true love, buy a pillow.

"FALL"ing Leaves

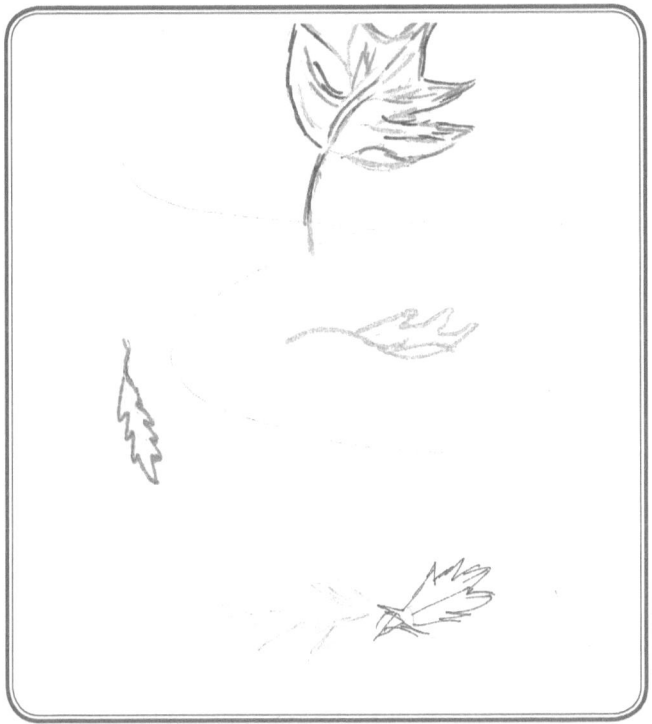

Oh the life that I have seen
I used to be so bright and green
Swaying in the sun and air
Without a worry or a care
But now I fall upon your head
No life to live because now I'm dead

Murdered Heart

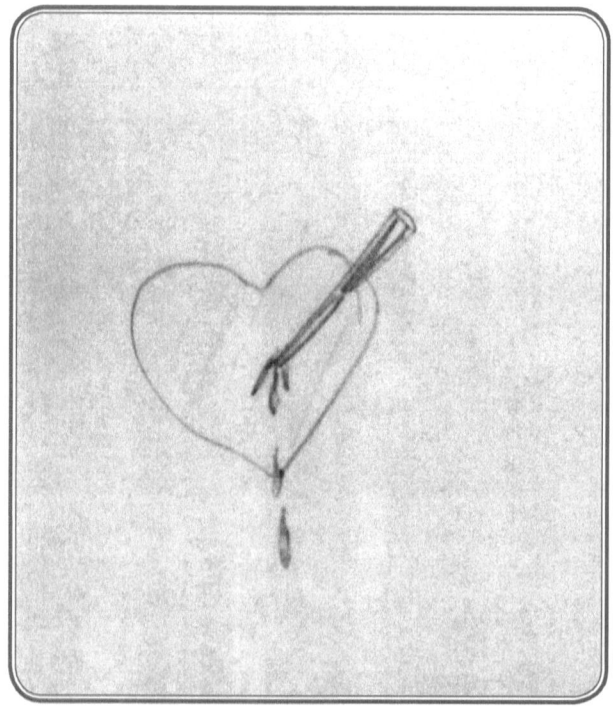

You came around and wore me down
Until I let you in
You jump the hurdles and climbed the wall
And I'll admit that I did fall
But with passing time
You did the crime
Of murdering my heart
Now I can't stay
Must be on my way
You know that we must part

Rosy Love

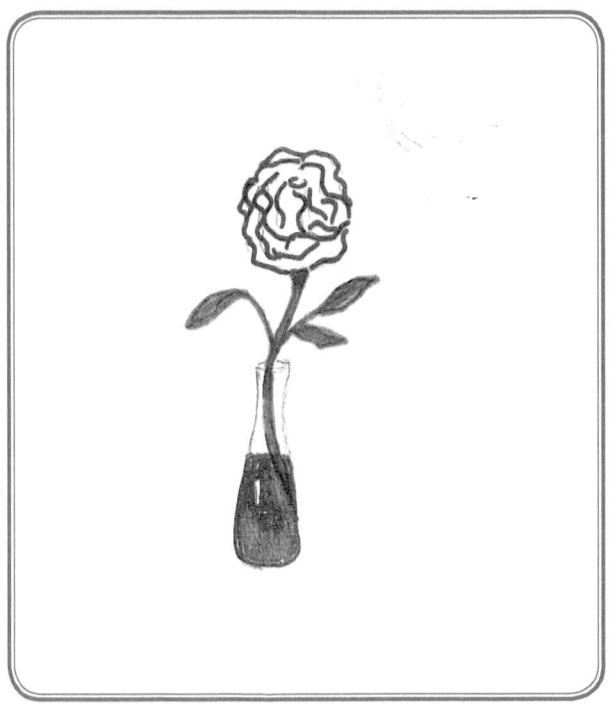

A relationship is like a rose;
How long it lasts, no one knows.
Love can erase an awful past;
Love can be yours, you'll see at last.
To feel that love, it makes you sigh;
To have it leave, you'd rather die.
You hope you've found that special rose
'Cause you love and care for the one you chose.

Mannequin

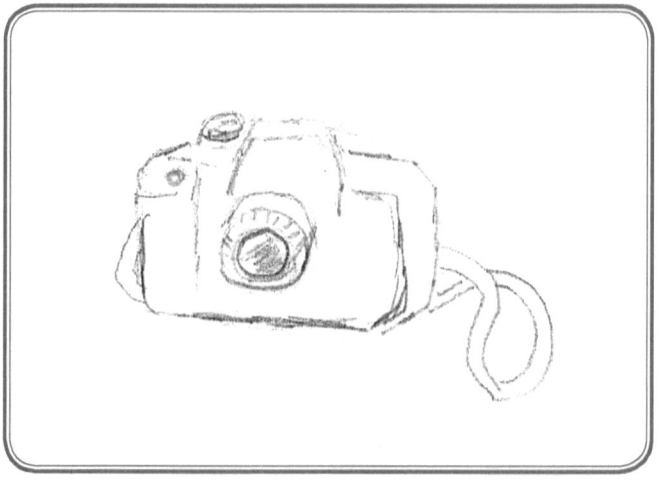

Freeze frame inside your mind,
Thoughts of perfection will I find.
To yourself, a story told;
For what you seek there is no mold.
In reality you live with doubt;
For that reason, you are without.
Freeze frame inside my mind,
Perfectly imperfect is what you'll find.

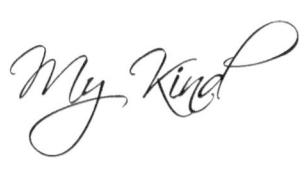

My Kind

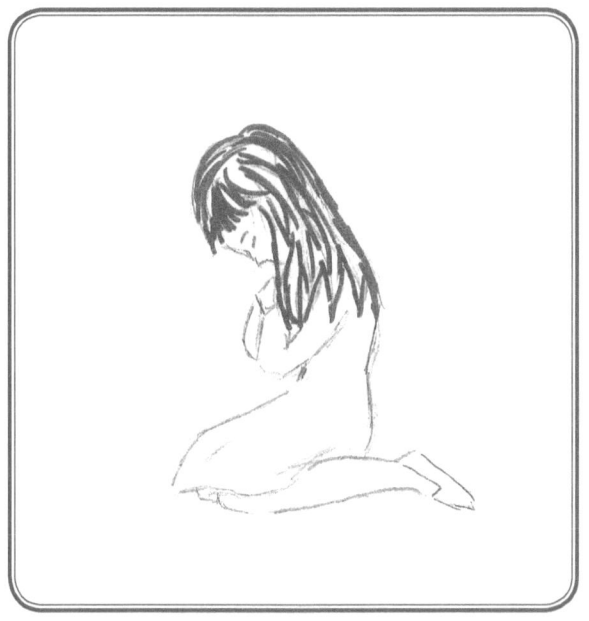

Do you think you know me?
Are you in my mind?
Can you read my heart?
Think you know *my kind*?
Did you know I'm human?
I'm just like you
I'm no angel; I sin every day
Fall short of HIS glory in every way
One thing that's different between me and you
I fall at God's feet, seeking mercy
Not sure what you do
I'm forgiven through Him, not by my deeds
So don't get it twisted while you're lost in the weeds

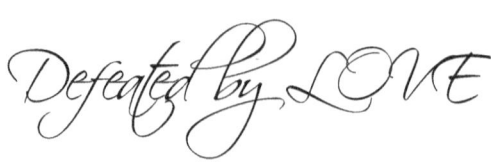

Defeated by LOVE

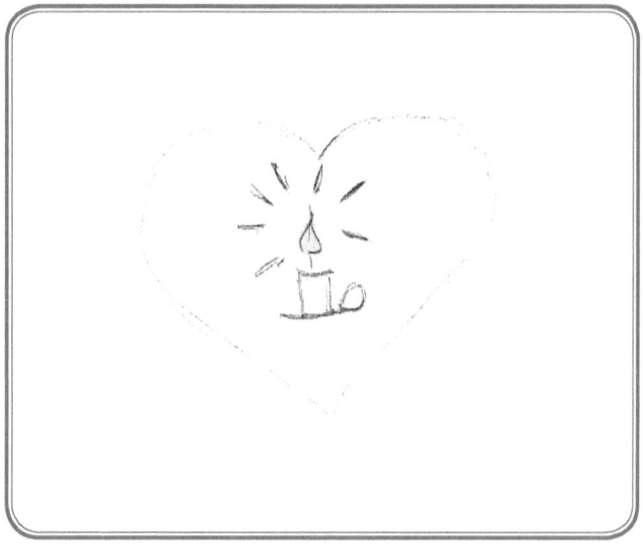

You've slowly unfolded your evil plan
Overloading the world with sin
A battle that starts within
You crushed and lied and filled us with pride
All while sitting behind the scenes
You've caused anger and strife over nothing
Even Mother Nature has now been stirred
Her birth pangs bring anguish to all
As we watch while our communities fall
You've shot your hate into innocent crowds
But our *INNER LIGHT* will always speak loud
Maybe you didn't read the Bible through
But the words within it are so very true
You have been conquered by the one above
All your hate and lies are defeated by *LOVE*

Where Art Thou, Spoon?

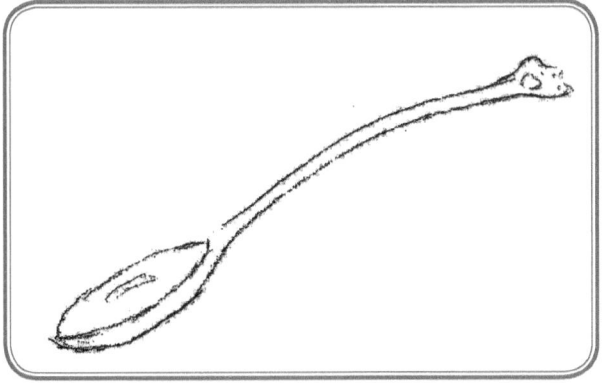

Flipping through a magazine
My hunger craves a nice cuisine
I whip me up a tasty treat
Only to face a terrible feat
My silver scoop has gone astray
Causing me so much dismay
I search frantic with all my might
Yet it still remains out of sight
Then just as I may lose my tune
I finally find my long-lost spoon

Just Ask

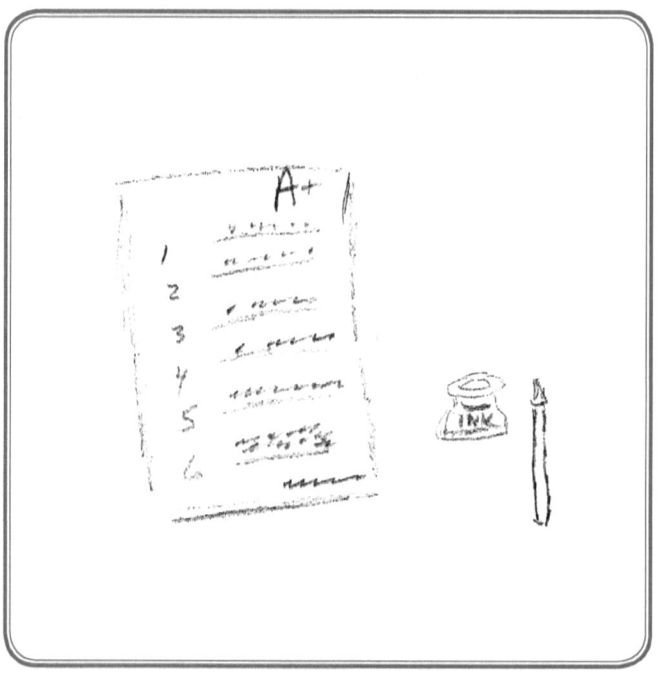

If you'd asked, I would say yes
But now I fear I may digress
I surely hope I passed your test
I tried to do my very best
Put in the hours of my time
But things can change on a dime
It can still turn out that way
But this moment will soon fade away

Beast Mode

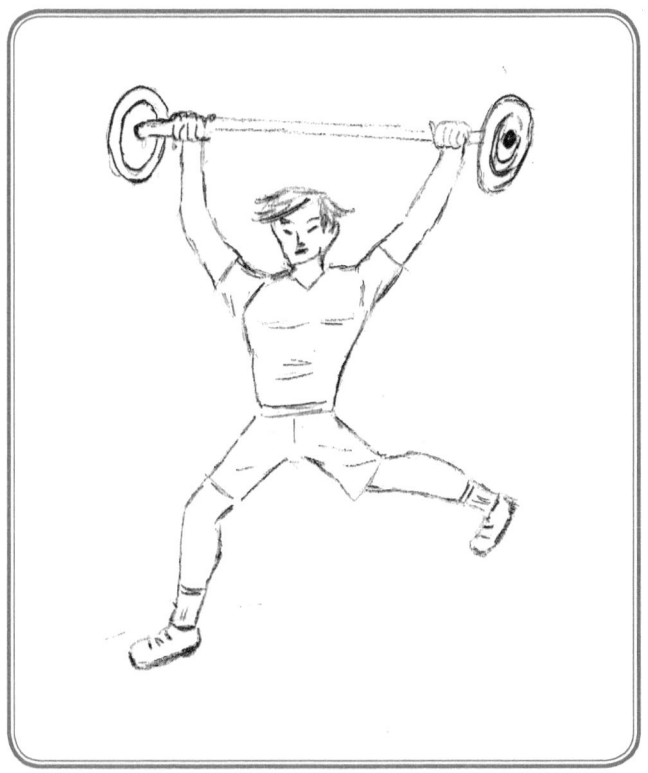

Cold iron in each hand
Pushing and pulling feels so grand
Sweating nothing but pure pain
Beast mode flowing in every vein
Grind to failure, but won't stop
Must keep going to be on top
My body is God's awesome gift
That is why I love to lift

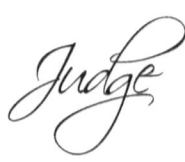

Judge

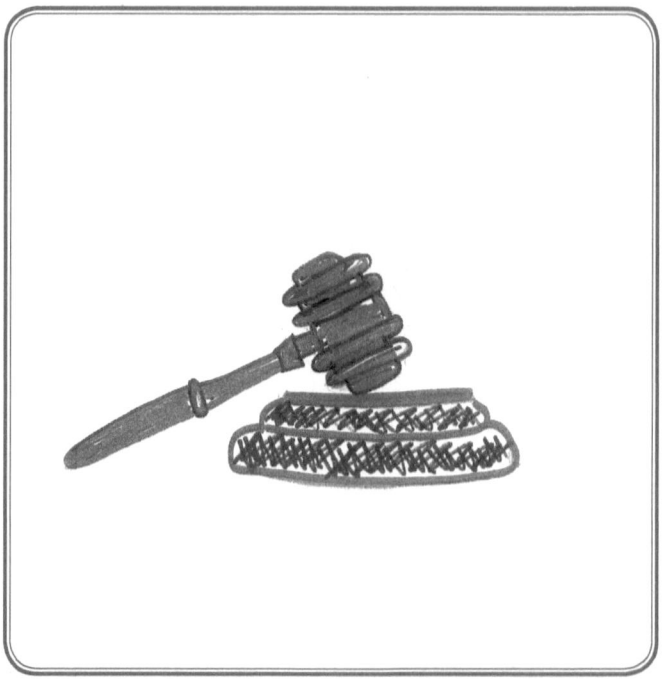

Don't be so quick to judge me
I'm a lot more than what you see
My layers are many; my love runs deep
My heart has felt much
The eyes tell the story
You'd be surprised, I'll tell you that
If you actually took the time to chat
Don't be so quick to judge me
I'm a lot more than what you see

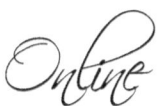

Online

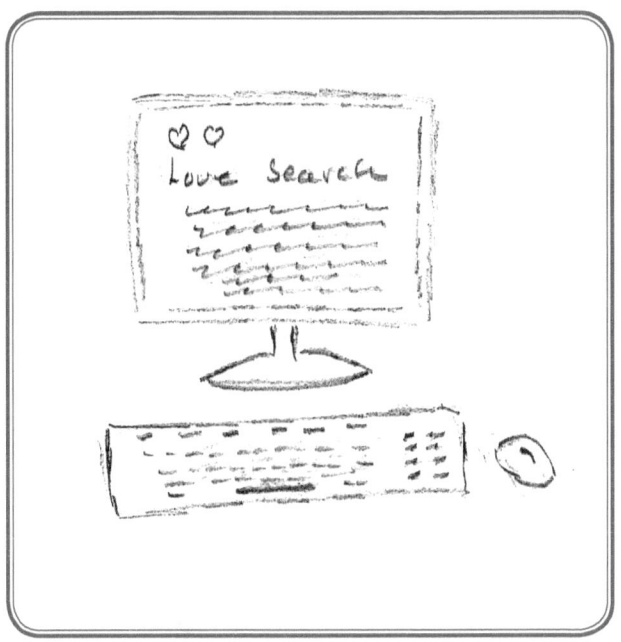

You're searching daily for the one
Looking everywhere under the sun
Scanning all the electronic files
Pictures of fakeness that goes on for miles
You say, "Why can't I find the one for me?"
"I'm always online, consistently"
Give it to God, just let it go
His will be done; this we know

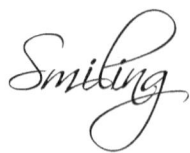

Smiling

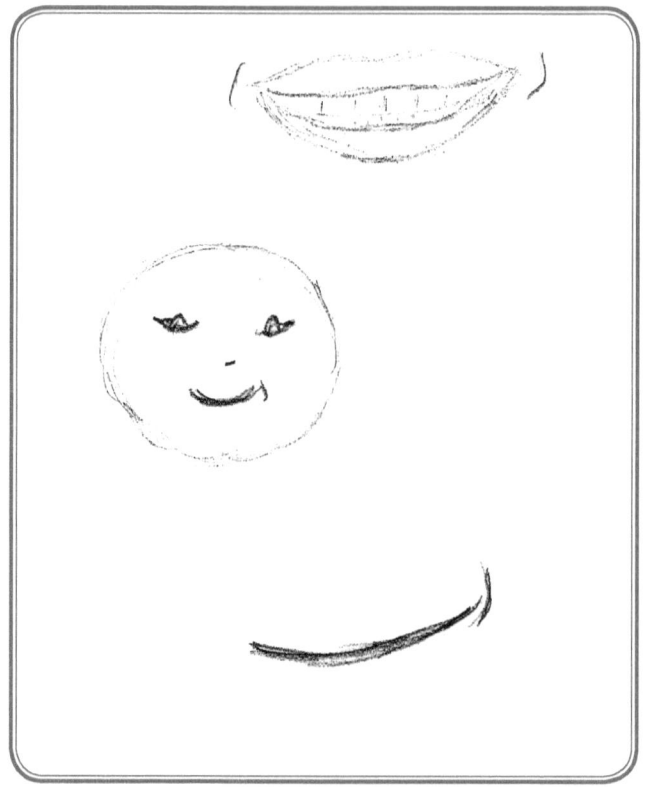

Smile is a language of love;
Smile is a source to win heart.
Smile is a name of lovely mood;
Smile creates greatness in personality,
So keep smiling.

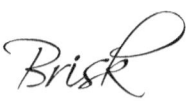

Brisk

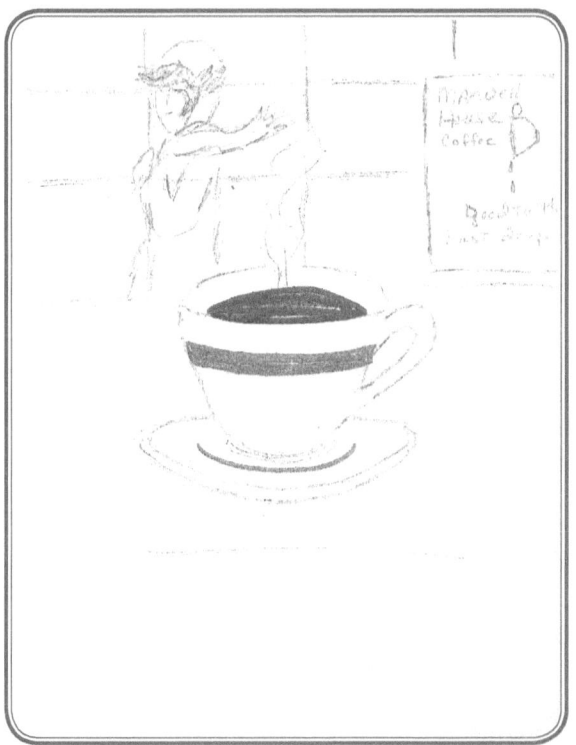

There is a chill in the air
As the day beats on my face
Cold wind is in my hair
In warmth I am wrapped
Fresh coffee has been tapped
Must face the day of gray
Till sunshine heads my way

Cloudy Tears

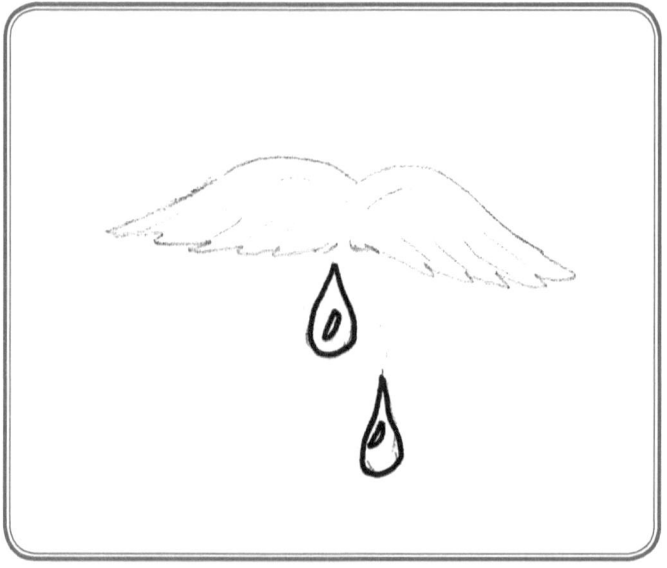

Rain falls like tears from the angels
Are they full of joy or filled with pain?
Mankind and life have gone insane
Full of greed and selfish gain
Hateful fighting, war, and grudge
Wanting nothing but peace and love
Yet so quick to point and judge
None willing to change
None willing to budge
So continues these troubled passing years
An eternal storm made of saddened angel tears

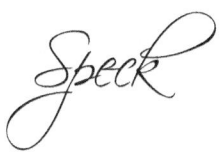

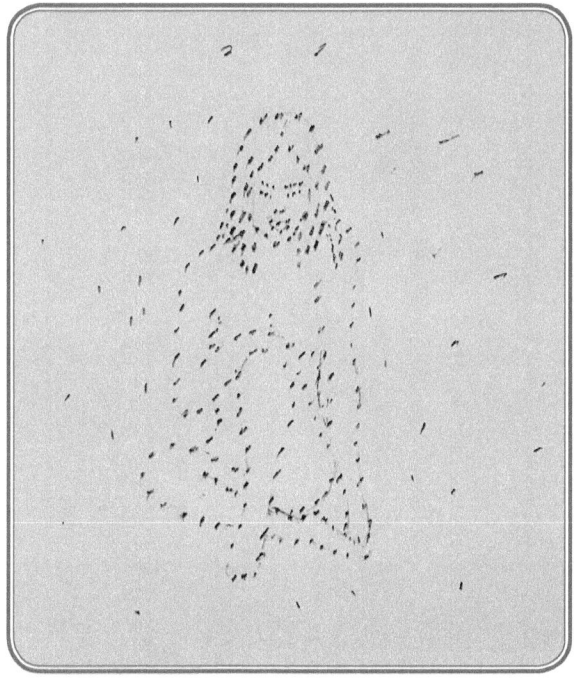

I am but a speck among a mass of dots
Looking for my meaning, floating in the same old spots
Only a beat of a larger heart
My mother and father gave me my start
Still searching for what sets me apart
Aiming at the target
Yet I have no dart

Night Dancing

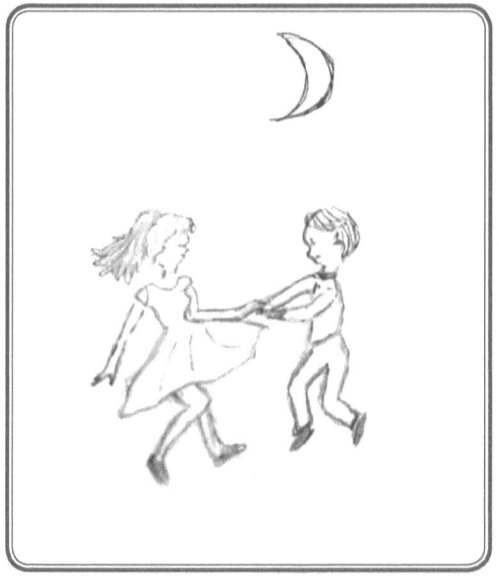

Look deep into my eyes
Sweep me off my feet
Dance with me into the night
Let's twirl to the beat
When morning comes, I must go
My name, my story, you'll never know
But for tonight we have this music
Tonight we dance!

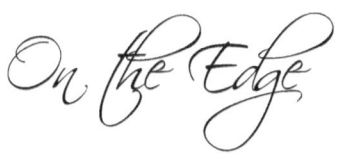

On the Edge

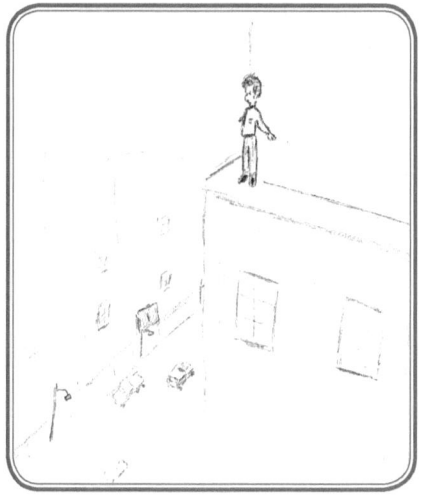

Another chapter has come to an end
The final pages still left blank
I won't break, but I may bend
Standing on the edge of this plank
What's below, I do not know
Don't want to jump … don't want to go
The world below looks so alone …

Yet here I am on the edge

Lord, hold my hand and hold it tight
Satan won't let go without a fight
If my plank should start to sway
I'll hit my knees and start to pray
For You know the remainder of my story
I only hope that it brings You glory …
Yet here I am on the edge

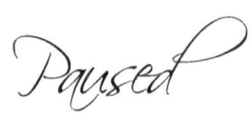

Paused

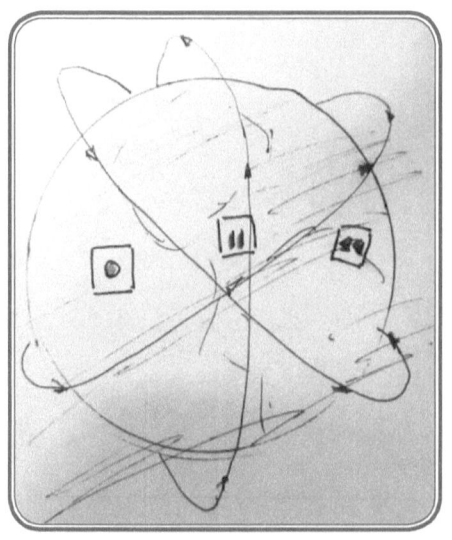

The world is full of so much commotion
Be still and know
Watch day seems to be in slow motion
Be still and know
You pushed the Stop button on our day
Be still and know
It's still we listen to what you have say

My child, tell me when you last prayed
Tell me when, like a child, you played
My child, tell me of an enemy you love
Tell me when you last sought me above
If creation follows only my commands
Why you trust in the work of *your hands*
You're lost on what to do or where to go
But I tell you, just ... be still and know

Just Be

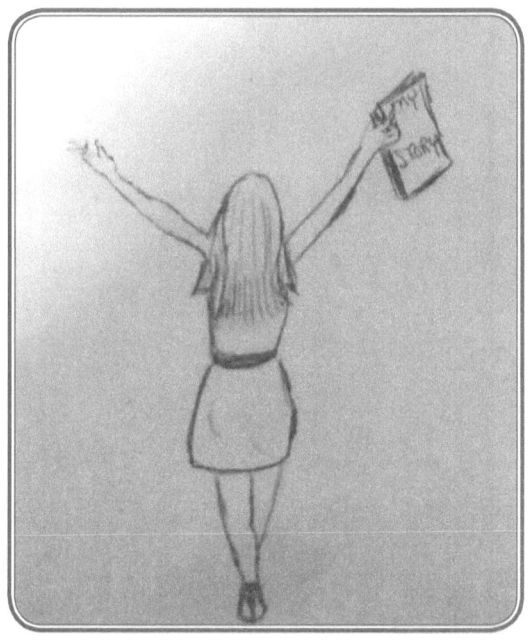

Life is too short to waste a moment
Staring into a looking glass
Wondering what soon will pass
Live your life in all its glory
Only you can write your own story
Wake each day with no resent
In all things, be fully present
Never rely on another person
Or hate in your heart will only worsen
Expectations can kill the soul
So focus on being truly complete; after all, that is the goal

You Are Worth More

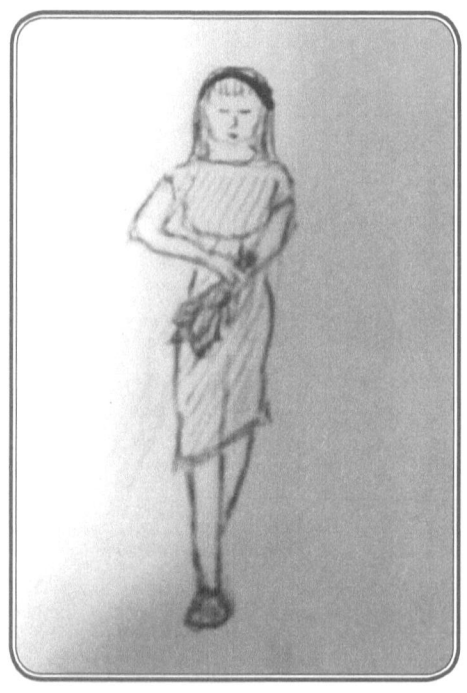

He said you were his forever
But her told her the same
He didn't know you'd be so clever
To catch him at his own game
Now wipe the memories from your eyes
Get up, dust off, get away from the lies
Don't turn back to try once more
You know it will only leave your heart sore
You are so much more; you deserve the best
Trust in God, put Him to the test
Walk away from the past; you know what to do
God has something better just waiting for you

Actions Louder than Words

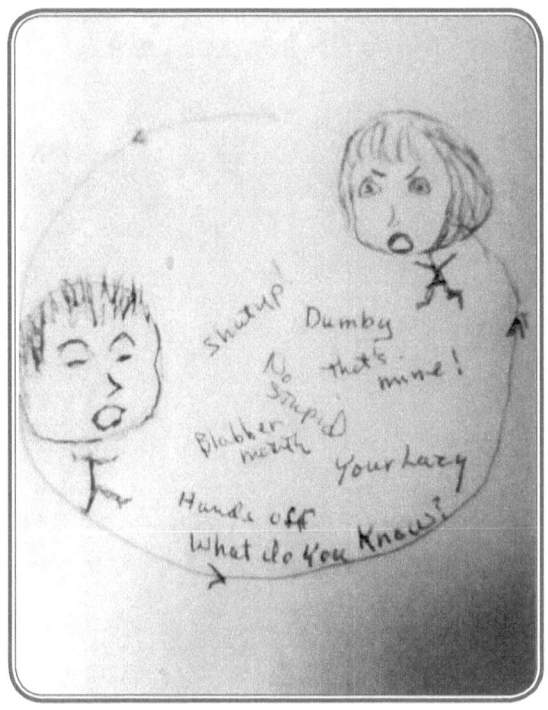

You talk too much; I say too much
Words vomit from our mouths
Can't set it free, won't leave it be
It cannot have control
Can talk the talk, but won't walk the walk
Running me in circles
Care to stare, a glassy glare
Don't blink or you may lose it
When all is said, lay down your head
Begin again tomorrow

The Judgmental

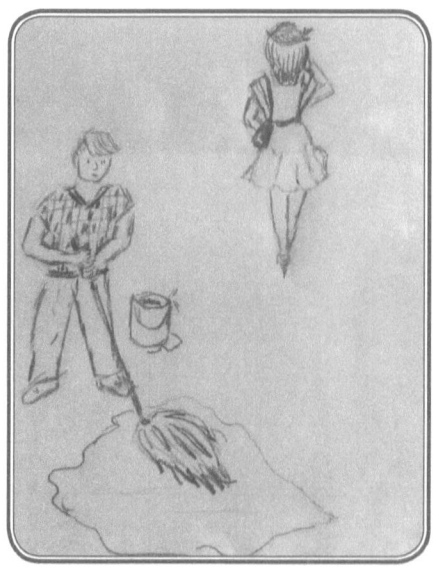

Living life without a care
For those who won't, it doesn't seem fair
Dancing in the sweet fall air
Others don't get it so they stop and stare
Placing themselves up high in a chair
Looking down in a snarling glare
Not knowing that they too could be there
I live my life with joyous flare
On my sleeve, my heart I do wear
Though at times mine too can tear
The beauty of life will always repair
If others would just try to share
If only they would even dare
The feeling they'd have would never compare
To living their lives up high in a chair

Strange Lover

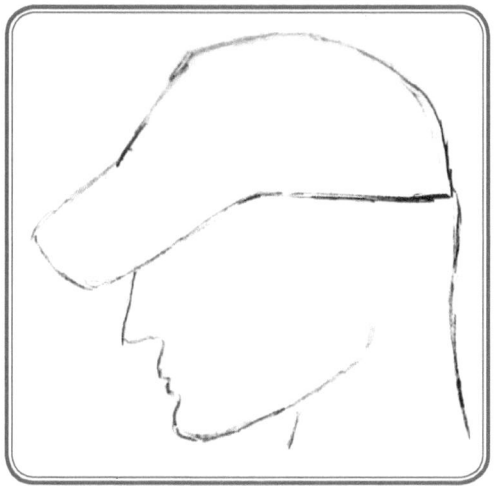

I close my eyes and can smell you
But I cannot see your face
I can feel your breath
But cannot touch your face
I can hear your voice
But your lips are not there
I can feel you, but you are not here
My heart races
Though you are not near
My mind is going insane
I do not know you
Not even your name

Unafraid

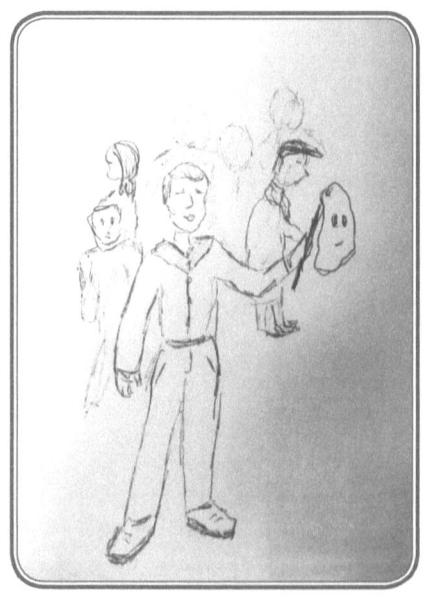

Appearing so close
Yet seeming so far
Afraid to show all that you are
In your past pain, you have grown
To fear every future unknown
And though amazing it may be
Your instinct is to quickly flee
Although it may be very hard
Because your heart has been scared
Let go of all control
Follow what's in your soul
Set all our fears free
Then so happy you will be

Love Us Anyway

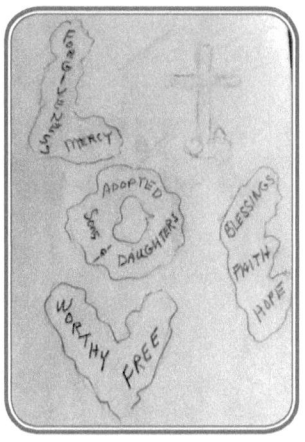

We came into the world with sin
Entered existence with it in our skin
Raised to think we can fix it alone
Is not what Bible verses condone
Christ came and looked on our curse
Or did you somehow skip that verse?
By dying to self, Christ lives within
His blood washes away all our sin
Showing your faith with each deed
It says have faith of a mustard seed
You say you have faith
Yet your mountain stays still
You're saved by faith, not your will
Know your identity in His eyes
The word He speaks never lies
You're His beloved child every day
But even if you don't believe what I say
God is going to love you anyway

Mind Me

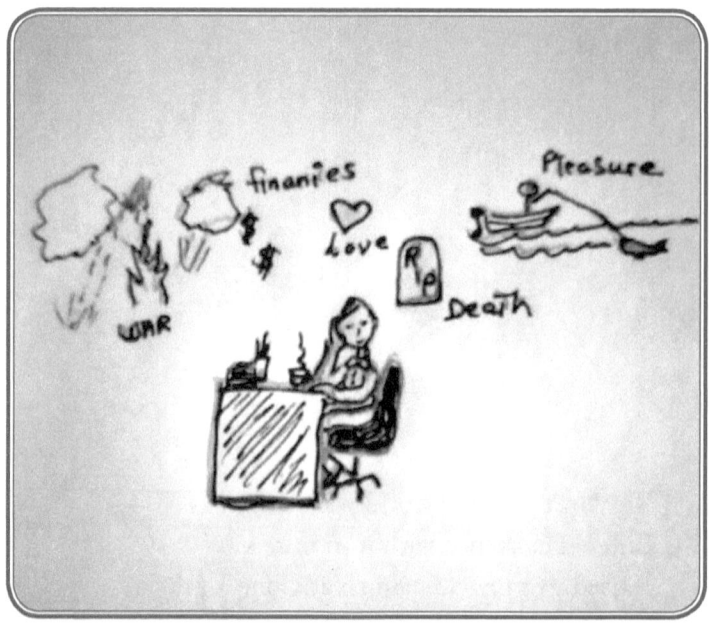

A million thoughts race through my mind
Flashing pictures of every kind
No words have been spoken
You mouth, it must be broken
Turmoil in my stomach's pit
In silence I continue to sit
A story in my mind I am told
Yet not knowing what will unfold
My out does not wear a smile
This has been going on for a while
Only time will let me see
Until then, don't mind me

Cracked but Not Broken

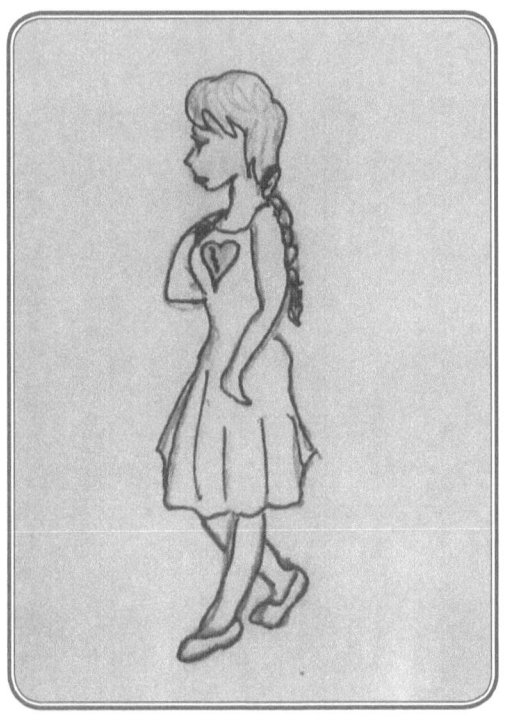

I've realized you will never see it
That thing I keep inside
I tried to show you all of it
But now it's something that I hide
It hurts me deep within my soul
To know this thing will never grow
I feel pain to see your face
When all I want is a warm embrace
Though it's hard, this I know
I must give it to God, must let it go